SOUTHERN STEAM RECOLLECTIONS

A PORTRAIT OF THE LAST YEARS

SOUTHERN STEAM RECOLLECTIONS

A PORTRAIT OF THE LAST YEARS

Don Benn

AN IMPRINT OF PEN & SWORD BOOKS LTD.
YORKSHIRE – PHILADELPHIA

First published in Great Britain in 2019 by
Pen and Sword Transport
An imprint of
Pen & Sword Books Ltd
Yorkshire - Philadelphia

Copyright © Don Benn, 2019

ISBN 978 1 52672 689 6

The right of Don Benn to be identified as Author of this work has been asserted by him in accordance with the Copyright, Designs and Patents Act 1988.

A CIP catalogue record for this book is available from the British Library.

All rights reserved. No part of this book may be reproduced or transmitted in any form or by any means, electronic or mechanical including photocopying, recording or by any information storage and retrieval system, without permission from the Publisher in writing.

Typeset by Aura Technology and Software Services, India
Printed and bound in India by Replika Press Pvt. Ltd.

Pen & Sword Books Ltd incorporates the Imprints of Pen & Sword Books Archaeology, Atlas, Aviation, Battleground, Discovery, Family History, History, Maritime, Military, Naval, Politics, Railways, Select, Transport, True Crime, Fiction, Frontline Books, Leo Cooper, Praetorian Press, Seaforth Publishing, Wharncliffe and White Owl.

For a complete list of Pen & Sword titles please contact

PEN & SWORD BOOKS LIMITED
47 Church Street, Barnsley, South Yorkshire, S70 2AS, England
E-mail: enquiries@pen-and-sword.co.uk
Website: www.pen-and-sword.co.uk

or

PEN AND SWORD BOOKS
1950 Lawrence Rd, Havertown, PA 19083, USA
E-mail: Uspen-and-sword@casematepublishers.com
Website: www.penandswordbooks.com

Contents

Introduction	6
South Eastern Lines	7
Central Lines	29
South Western Lines	89
Acknowledgements	157
Bibliography	158

Introduction

I started taking photographs of steam locomotives and steam hauled trains on the Southern in 1960 and continued until the end of steam in July 1967. The quality of most of the very early photographs isn't good enough for reproduction, but better cameras enabled improved images to be obtained during the most prolific years of 1961 to 1963 which fortunately enabled the last of the classic ex Southern Railway designs, such as the King Arthurs, Lord Nelson and Schools classes to be captured for posterity. This book contains 150 black and white photographs ranging across the Southern Region starting in the east and then moving gradually westwards to include a few taken on the 'withered arm' in Cornwall. Most though are taken in the areas just south and south-west of London and include once popular locations such as the footpaths at South Croydon and Wimbledon. Trains like the Bournemouth Belle and the Schools class hauled 5.25 pm London Bridge to Reading and Lymington Pier boat trains are shown to good effect. Most of the photographs are previously unpublished and this book will appeal to all Southern devotees. I have tried to make this photo album interesting by using extended captions which are linked one to another as far as possible and in doing so I have had to dig deep in my memory and into my records, which fortunately from about September 1961 are quite detailed. My collection of Southern timetables has also proved to be invaluable. Other sources are shown in the Bibliography.

South Eastern Lines

From 1950 until August 1961 the family lived in Bromley and it wasn't long before I found my way to the footbridge over the lines at Bromley North. Here a C class 0-6-0 shunted the then quite extensive yard every weekday. I still have clear memories of the engine pulling a long rake of wagons and vans up the headshunt which stretched nearly to Sundridge Park station before performing a fly shunting movement with the shunter running alongside the wagons to apply the brakes. In this shot taken in October 1960, No. 31690 rests by the footbridge between duties.

Also within walking distance through footpaths was the bridge over the Charing Cross to Ashford and Dover main line near Elmstead Woods tunnel on the 1-in-120 climb out of London to the North Downs. This became a favourite spot and here C class 0-6-0 No. 31573 struggles uphill with a heavy freight in November 1960. I would lie in bed at night and listen to the slow slogging of such engines fighting the gradient with heavy freights which could be heard quite clearly though the line was some distance away.

The C class engines also shunted the small up yard at Bromley South. 31579 was built at Ashford in October 1903 and was therefore nearly 58 years old when photographed in June 1961 during the last week of steam operation. The old footbridge over the county end of the station, from the steps of which this shot was taken, was another favourite venue for watching and photographing trains, and from this bridge I witnessed the last evening of steam between Victoria and Ramsgate/Dover via Chatham on 14th June 1959, it being usurped by the Cep electric units, one of which can be seen in the background of this shot on an up train.

The branch line from Dunton Green to Westerham survived beyond the end of main line steam and was much visited in the years before closure by train or bus to Downe and then a long walk. The friendly loco crews were used to enthusiasts being around and cab visits were common. This shot taken in May 1961 shows the view from the cab of Wainwright H class 0-4-4 tank No. 31543, a Tonbridge based loco built in January 1909 and one which frequently worked the service. It survived until July 1963 working trains on Central Division lines.

The H class tanks monopolised the service in the last couple of years of operation and No. 31177 was another frequent visitor. Here it is seen near Brasted on Tonbridge Duty 238 in August 1961. We would often walk the line in the quest for good locations to photograph the push-pull worked trains which always had the engine facing Westerham. We didn't have lineside permits but nobody seemed to worry in those far off days on a line which was doomed.

On the same day as the previous photograph, 31177 sits in the sun at the Westerham terminus having arrived from Dunton Green. After the 4.5 mile line closed on 28th October 1961 it was the subject of an abortive preservation attempt which finally failed in 1964 when Kent County Council used part of the line for the Sevenoaks bypass and financial backers for reinstating the line withdrew. British Railways had planned to electrify the line but the Transport Minister agreed to closure. Nothing remains of the terminus but the goods yard and approach road at Brasted still exist next to the M25.

One week before closure and on the final Sunday of operation on 22nd October 1961, H class 0-4-4 tank No. 31263 is seen near Brasted with a train from Dunton Green. Sunday was the only day when trains ran all day right up to the 9.50 pm from Dunton Green, whereas the Monday to Friday service was geared to commuters and on Saturdays there was a gap in service for most of the morning after the early trains. After closure No. 31263 worked trains on the Central Division including between Three Bridges to East Grinstead (See pages 81 and 82) before being withdrawn in January 1964 and is now preserved on the Bluebell Railway in SECR colours.

A train which attracted a lot of attention in 1961 was the 7.24 am London Bridge to Ramsgate via Tonbridge, Ashford and Dover. The train started as empty stock from Holborn Viaduct and due to a weight restriction it had to be hauled by an engine with a light axle loading and this invariably was one of the remaining Bricklayers Arms based Maunsell 4-4-0s, either D1 or E1 classes, although very occasionally a C class 0-6-0 would be substituted. Here E1 class No. 31507 is approaching Elmstead Woods tunnel during the last week of steam in June 1961.

The complex of junctions in the Chislehurst and Petts Wood areas was just within walking distance and provided ample opportunity to see remaining steam working on both the South Eastern and Chatham main lines by dodging between the two. This shot is taken at St Mary Cray Junction where N class 2-6-0 No. 31404 is crossing from the down fast to the down slow line with a freight train in April 1961. The headcode discs suggest a train from Bricklayers Arms to Dover via Chislehurst and Maidstone East. 31404 was an Ashford based engine.

Over on the South Eastern main line at Petts Wood Junction, Stewarts Lane based N class 2-6-0 No. 31412 is heading an up Engineers train on the fast line, probably destined for Hither Green sidings via Chislehurst. This shot was also taken in April 1961. Although we could walk to the line here, we would sometimes catch a train from Bromley South to Petts Wood from where this junction was a short walk.

On the same day at the same location as the previous shot, Schools class 4-4-0 No. 30928 *Stowe* is on the up slow line with a three coach Hastings line set working empty stock from Tonbridge to London. This train would have set out on the 5.45 am from London Bridge to Hastings via Tunbridge Wells, continuing at 8.34 am to Ashford. After arrival it would have worked the 9.30 am stopping train to Tonbridge. 30928 was one of the very successful class of Maunsell designed locos introduced in 1934 and was withdrawn in November 1962 but is preserved on the Bluebell Railway.

Moving back now to Bromley South, this time from platforms one and two on a very wet day in May 1961, we see No. 34061 *73 Squadron* in original condition travelling fast on an up boat train, probably the morning service from Paris via Calais, Folkestone Harbour and the main line via Tonbridge. This was timed to pass Bromley South at about 4 pm. On the right is my younger brother Bryan who was with me on most of my expeditions to see steam in action before it finished in June that year. Although based at Dover at the time, 34061 didn't feature often in my notes and was an early withdrawal in June 1964.

On a day of very different weather earlier in May 1961, the same train is passing Bromley South on the more usual up fast line. The engine in charge is rebuilt West Country class No. 34101 *Hartland*, a frequent performer and looking to be in good nick with a safety valve just feathering and the driver relaxing with the job almost done. It's difficult to believe that steam only had about a month to run on the boat trains. 34101 went on to work trains on the South Western Division and I travelled 808 miles behind it before its withdrawal in July 1966.

Despite it being a cold and wet day, the first signs of spring are showing in March 1961 as No. 34004 *Yeovil* approaches Bickley on the 1-in-95 climb with a down afternoon boat train via Tonbridge and Folkestone Harbour. The train is on the down slow line so will need to cross over at Bickley Junction before diving under the lines to and from Charing Cross to gain the Tonbridge route. It was more normal for boat trains to use the down fast from Shortlands Junction to Bickley Junction. 34004 went to Eastleigh at the end of May 1961 and lasted right to the end of steam on 9th July 1967.

Back at Bromley South and on the more usual down fast line, No. 34077 *603 Squadron* is heading a morning boat train. It's a beautiful sunny but cold Sunday, 12th February 1961, and the train is routed via Chatham due to engineering works in the Petts Wood area. No. 34077 was a frequent performer on the boat trains as we shall see with the next few shots and it was transferred to Nine Elms on 26th May 1961 to work on the Bournemouth line. Unfortunately unlike 34101 it had a reputation for poor steaming so I avoided it when out travelling behind steam.

St Mary Cray Junction in April 1961 is the location for another shot of No. 34077. It is working an up afternoon boat train which had operated via Maidstone East. This location was transformed with Phase One of the Kent Coast electrification in June 1959. Before that this section was two tracks and I remember there being a footpath crossing in the far distance of this shot where we used to place pennies on the line to be squashed by the passing steam hauled trains. The crossing was replaced by a subway. On the right is the single up line joining the Chatham route to the Charing Cross route at Chislehurst.

34077 again this time working a down boat train via Chatham in April 1961. The shot is taken from the steps of the footbridge from where the previous shot was taken. Some years before, probably in about 1958, we were just arriving at this location on the footpath from Chislehurst on a hot summer day when we spied a Midland Region interloper standing at the junction signals having come round the loop from Chislehurst. It was none other than 5XP Jubilee No. 45602 *British Honduras* on a through train from the Midland Region and was blowing off furiously, possibly waiting for permission to proceed as Jubilees were banned from working on the Chatham route!

Taken on the other side of the footbridge and showing the path from Chislehurst, *603 Squadron* is working a down boat train via Maidstone East on a bright day in April 1961. We would sometimes catch an RF bus on Service 227 from Market Square, Bromley to Chislehurst Station or Common before walking along tracks and footpaths to the footbridge. An abiding memory of this location is of a C class 0-6-0 storming along at a good speed with a 15-coach train of empty pigeon vans on the up line. Sammy Gingell driving maybe?

I must have been out taking photos a lot in April 1961 as here is another one on a bright spring day taken from the bridge in the approach to Elmstead Woods tunnel. It shows No. 34025 *Whimple* on the 9.10 am Charing Cross to Ramsgate train, one of only a few ordinary service trains lasting until June 1961. This and other photos of the same engine at that time confirm the absence of a West Country class crest. The engine was originally named *Rough Tor* for a short time in 1948. At the time this shot was taken it was based at Bricklayers Arms and was one of a number of locos moved to the South Western Division, in this case Eastleigh, on 26th May 1961. It lasted until the end of steam on 9th July 1967 and was rostered for Nine Elms Duty 254 on Friday, 7th July, the 5.23 pm Waterloo to Bournemouth, one of the last down steam hauled trains.

No book of mine about Southern steam would ever be complete without at least one image of the Golden Arrow. I saw this train many hundreds of times from the very early days on the footbridge at Bromley South until the end of steam on South Eastern main lines. I can recall seeing it hauled by Bulleid Merchant Navy pacific No. 35001 *Channel Packet* in its original condition and by rebuilt 35015 *Rotterdam Lloyd* on 13th June 1959 for instance and by 35028 *Clan Line* on 4th July 1959 according to my notebooks. Also by the two magnificent Stewarts Lane based Britannia pacifics No. 70004 *William Shakespeare* and No.70014 *Iron Duke*. This shot however shows the engine which was almost always on the train during its last few months of steam haulage, No. 34100 *Appledore*. It is running on time at about 7.25 pm on its usual up Chatham line at Bromley South in June 1961. The footbridge no longer exists, being replaced by a wide road bridge.

During the last week of steam, with the collusion of my house master I bunked off school a couple of times to get shots of the down 'Arrer'. This is my all time favourite shot of the train, in Bickley cutting headed as usual by No. 34100 *Appledore*. This location is barely changed since 1961 but the train has gone and my old Bromley Grammar School is now a renamed Comprehensive. 34100 moved to Brighton where it worked some of the remaining steam hauled trains on the Central Division, including the heavy 6.10 pm Victoria to Brighton via Oxted and then to Salisbury in 1963, where it lasted until the end of steam in 1967.

The final shot on South Eastern lines is of Schools class 4-4-0 No. 30926 *Repton* at Ashford shed on a very cold and snowy 25th February 1962 ready to work the Kentish Venturer railtour from Appledore to Charing Cross. The engine was in fine condition as driver Kennett showed by reaching 79 mph after Headcorn during a dash across the Weald of Kent in the dusk and snow, averaging 76.6 mph from Headcorn to Paddock Wood. 30926 was built at Eastleigh in 1934 and worked Waterloo to Portsmouth trains until 1937 when it went to Bournemouth. It was withdrawn from Basingstoke shed with the great cull of Southern Railway locomotives at the end of 1962 but is now preserved on the North Yorkshire Moors Railway.

Central Lines

After the end of steam on South Eastern lines I transferred my interest to Central and South Western lines in the London area. The family moved from Bromley to Shirley, Croydon, at about the same time and so whole new areas were opened up for exploration. I also acquired my first 35mm camera which was soon put to work. The weather at the end of September 1961 was fine and so I undertook a trip to Clapham Junction by train where on Friday 29th September I photographed BR Standard class four 2-6-4 tank No. 80081 storming through on the 10.38 am Victoria to Brighton and Eastbourne, fast to East Croydon and Oxted. The train has two Maunsell three coach sets and after the train divided at Eridge the rear set would be attached to the 11.10 am from Tonbridge to Eastbourne. This train was one of only two per day which followed this pattern. (see page 32 for the other).

On a more normal stopping pattern train and part of the eight minutes past each hour standard hourly service, BR Standard class four 2-6-4 tank No. 80015 is slowing for its Clapham Junction stop on the 3.08 pm Victoria to Tunbridge Wells West via Oxted. This train has a Maunsell three coach set strengthened with another Maunsell coach and a BR Mark One. The shed plate shows the engine to be based at 75F, Tunbridge Wells West. I travelled on this train to East Croydon, where I walked to South Croydon and continued to take photographs on a warm evening, including the one shown on page 40. 80015 was built at Brighton in 1951 and lasted right to the end of steam in 1967. On Friday, 7th July, it was allocated to Nine Elms Duty 101, empty stock and shunting work.

My selection of photos from Central Division lines continues on a broadly geographical basis, rather than chronological, and so the next shot is taken near Wandsworth Common. On a rare fine summer day in 1963, Sunday, 23rd June, Maunsell N class 2-6-0 No. 31825 is heading towards London with the empty stock for the 10.30 am Victoria to Newhaven Harbour. The smart MK One stock behind the engine is in contrast to the loco's filthy state. 31825 was allocated to Stewarts Lane shed and this was to close to steam in September 1963, so no doubt engine cleaning was a low priority, in contrast to the situation just two years before. This heavy train of 11 coaches and two 4 wheeled vans would total about 430 tons full but that would not be a problem for the electric locomotive, or one for the remaining Stewarts Lane West Country class pacific which would provide the power for the 80 minute run to Newhaven.

Once past Clapham Junction the Central Division main line to Brighton ran through some nice open spaces of which the one at Wandsworth Common was seen in the previous shot. Just beyond Balham is Tooting Bec Common, from which trains could be photographed from both sides. Here BR Standard class four 4-6-0 No. 75074 is working the 3.54 pm Victoria to Brighton on 21st June 1963. This was the other train referred to on page 29 which conveyed through carriages for Eastbourne, being attached to the 4.08 pm from Tonbridge at Eridge, and arrived at Eastbourne at 6.13pm. The rolling stock is two Bulleid three coach sets. The train was a regular turn for a Stewarts Lane based BR Standard class four 4-6-0.

Most Oxted line trains were hauled by the very successful Riddles designed BR Standard class four 2-6-4 tanks. Passing Tooting Bec Common on a bright but cold 4th February 1962 is 80137 on the 10.08 am Victoria to Tunbridge Wells West. The engine was shedded at Tunbridge Wells at the time the shot was taken but moved to Brighton in 1963 before withdrawal in October 1965, a scandalously short life as it wasn't built until 1956.

The early 1960s were enhanced by railtours using combinations of steam locos which could not be contemplated today. Taken from the other side of the line at Tooting Bec Common on a beautifully warm 15th September 1963 is the 'The Blue Belle' railtour (proper name 'The Scottish Belle 3') which ran from Victoria to Haywards Heath and returned with the astonishing combination of Caledonian single 4-2-2 No. 123 and LSWR T9 class 4-4-0 No.120. They were passing me at 11.25 am. At Haywards Heath LSWR Adams 4-4-2 tank No. 488 and LBSCR E4 class 0-6-2 tank No. 473 took the train to Horsted Keynes where SECR P class 0-6-0 tank No. 27 took the whole train to Sheffield Park. It returned to Horsted Keynes with LBSCR Terrier tank No. 55 and then continued back to London with the same locos as the outward journey. I photographed it passing South Croydon at 6.06 pm.

Norwood Junction shed (75C) was close to where we lived and easy to photograph and bunk as there was a footbridge over the line from Crystal Palace to Norwood Junction station which led down to the shed. The shed foreman also seemed to be a tolerant character and I don't remember ever being thrown out despite often wandering amongst the locos moving around the yard. In 1961 its allocation of locos were mainly used on freight work in the area. Sitting in the sunshine on 7th October 1961 is Q class 0-6-0 No. 30549. It was built in September 1939 and lasted until July 1963.

The allocation of steam locos at Norwood Junction in 1961 included W class 2-6-4 tanks and C2X class 0-6-0s. Here W class No. 31914 is coming off shed while C2X No. 32549 is waiting its next turn. Also on shed that day, 7th October 1961, was C2X No. 32547. Both engines were introduced in 1902 and withdrawn in November 1961. N Class 2-6-0 No. 31825 and C class 0-6-0 No. 31717 were working freights in the area that day.

This shot was taken near West Croydon on Saturday, 4th November 1961, and shows C2X class 0-6-0 No. 32549 working a freight on the line from Sutton having just passed Waddon. This must have been one of the locos last workings as it was withdrawn a few days later. I saw its sister C2X No. 32547 working a freight at Purley on 18th November and possibly both locos were withdrawn soon after that, leaving just two survivors of the class at Three Bridges shed until January 1962. The line curving of to the right is the one to Wimbledon and this is now part of the Croydon Tramlink which crosses the Sutton line on a flyover, transforming this scene.

Just a couple of miles away is the very busy station of East Croydon, the buildings of which can be seen spanning the main road bridge in the background. It's Sunday 5th August 1962 and I was there primarily to see if any through train from the Midlands to Brighton would appear that day, as on most summer Sundays. They did, hauled by rebuilt West Country class pacific No. 34100 *Appledore* and LM Class 5 4-6-0 No. 45314 plus Type 2 DL No. D5087. I also grabbed this shot of the 10.08 am Victoria to Tunbridge Wells West hauled by BR Standard class four 2-6-4 tank No. 80081, which is also featured on pages 29 and 45.

Another much visited location was South Croydon, where shots could be taken from the footpath next to the line, from the road overbridge at the end of the footpath or from the footbridge over the north end of the station. This shot of N class 2-6-0 No. 31411 working the 1.55 pm Brighton to Victoria on Saturday 21st October 1961 was taken from the footpath. During the week this train would be hauled by a Brighton based West Country class pacific which would return on the heavy 6.10 pm Victoria to Brighton.(see page 42).

In 1961-62 the 5.25 pm London Bridge to Reading was a regular turn for a Brighton based Schools class 4-4-0. It ran nonstop to Coulsdon South and then stations to Reading via Redhill and Guildford. No. 30915 *Brighton* is approaching South Croydon on the warm and sunny evening of Friday 29th September 1961, going well and on time at 5.41 pm. I took many photos of this train as I worked in Croydon at the time though not so many of the up working which was the 7.27 am from Reading due London Bridge at 9.50 am.

Another shot of the 5.25 pm London Bridge, this time taken from the footpath and again on a nice sunny evening, Tuesday, 17 April 1962. In charge of the 10 coach train was No. 30930 *Radley* which had been transferred from Bricklayers Arms to Brighton with the great turnout of 26th May 1961. It lasted until December 1962 when it was withdrawn together with all its remaining class members, a sad end to a very fine class of steam locos. My obsession with photographing this train even extended to taking flash shots after dark such as on 26th January 1962 when No. 30916 *Whitgift* worked the train, but results weren't very successful.

The other evening train which attracted a lot of my attention was the 6.10 pm Victoria to Brighton via Oxted service. It was worked by a Brighton based West Country class pacific in 1962 and here No. 34101 Hartland is approaching South Croydon on 8th May 1962. This 11 coach train would tax even the power of a Bulleid pacific on the 1-in-100 climb to the tunnel at Woldingham before dropping down to Oxted where the train would divide, the front portion going forward to Brighton and the rear to Eastbourne via Heathfield and Polegate.

At South Croydon the steam worked Oxted line left the Brighton main line and climbed the steep 1-in-83 to Selsdon station. The part of this station used by Oxted line trains closed in 1959 but access to the platforms was still possible from the Woodside branch which lasted until 1983. Some spectacular shots of down trains were possible from the Oxted line platforms as here with BR Standard class four 2-6-4 tank No. 80143 on the 1.08 pm Victoria to Tunbridge Wells West taken on Thursday, 15th March 1962.

The next two shots were taken on a very cold but sunny Saturday, 13th January 1962. In this photo BR Standard class four 2-6-4 tank No. 80016 waits for the road onto the main line with the 9.24 am Tunbridge Wells West to Victoria train, while sister engine No. 80018 climbs past with the 10.08 am Victoria to Tunbridge Wells West. The 9.24 am was an extra service to fill a gap before the start of the standard off peak pattern.

After half an hour the next down train, the 10.38 am Victoria to Brighton, appeared hauled by No. 80081. This train was one of the two at 38 minutes past the hour from Victoria which ran fast to East Croydon and Oxted and divided at Eridge with portions for Brighton and Eastbourne. The trains at 8 minutes past each hour called at Clapham Junction, East Croydon then all stations to Tunbridge Wells West via East Grinstead.

Carrying on south on the main line we come to the old bridge over the line at the now closed Coulsdon North station where trains for both the Quarry line and the one via Merstham could be photographed. By 1963 there weren't many steam hauled trains on these lines but on summer Sundays and bank holidays through trains ran from the Midlands to Brighton and these were mainly steam hauled with 'foreign' engines. On a very hot Sunday, 2nd June 1963, LM Black Five 4-6-0 No. 45379 is heading one such train of 10 coaches, including three looking very smart. The time is 11.25 am. 45379 was built in 1937, withdrawn in 1965 and is now preserved on the Mid Hants Railway. It was based at Crewe North in 1963.

At Redhill the lines east to Tonbridge and west to Guildford and Reading were steam worked until the end of 1964 and I spent a lot of time on both in the early 1960s. Often I would travel by train from East Croydon such as on Sunday 8th December 1963 when I had arrived on the 10.46 am train with 4 Lav units 2936 and 2943 and travelled to Guildford behind U class 2-6-0 No. 31806 on the 11.36 am train returning from Guildford behind U class No. 31622 on the 12.55 pm before taking this shot of U class 2-6-0 No. 31797 sitting in the sun on the 2.05 pm to Guildford and Reading. I then returned to East Croydon on the 2.15 pm in a train comprised of 2 Bil and Hal units. 31797 was built at Ashford in 1928 and withdrawn in January 1964. It was based at Guildford MPD.

The Redhill to Guildford line was within cycling distance and this is how I managed to get most of my many shots from the lineside. The foot crossing on the Reigate side of Betchworth station was one of my favourite spots and here we see U class 2-6-0 No. 31626 on the 11.05 am Reading to Redhill service pulling away from its Betchworth stop on Saturday, 2nd November 1963. It was a mild day with the mercury standing at 63 degrees Farenheight, but still cool enough for nice smoke effects. The train is comprised of four Maunsell Hastings line coaches.

Facing the other way at the same crossing on Good Friday, 20th April 1962, U class 2-6-0 No. 31610 is in charge of a BR MK 1 three coach set on the 2.05pm Redhill to Reading. 31610 was the first of Maunsell's U class Moguls and was built at Brighton in 1928. It was the second one to be withdrawn, in December 1962, leaving 48 of the 50 locos still in service. At the time the photo was taken it was shedded at Guildford.

This shot was taken the next day, Easter Saturday, 21st April 1962, from the road next to Betchworth station. It shows Redhill based N class 2-6-0 No. 31868 on the heavy 12 coach Margate, Dover, Eastbourne and Brighton to Wolverhampton through train. The corresponding 10.50 am Wolverhampton to Margate and Dover train consisted of 13 coaches and was hauled by Schools class 4-4-0 No. 30930 *Radley*. By the time that appeared at 3 pm it was raining and cold so I soon cycled home arriving very wet and woke the next day with a cold.

Conditions were very different on Monday 8th July 1963 when I photographed N class 2-6-0 No. 31858 topping Gomshall summit with the 9.45 am Reading to Redhill train. The mogul was hauling four Maunsell flat sided Hastings line coaches. My book *Biography of British Train Travel*, published by Pen & Sword, contains a 26 page chapter on the Redhill to Guildford line with photos and train running logs.

Back now to Sanderstead to continue south on the Oxted line. The date is Saturday 13th October 1962 and W class 2-6-4 tank No. 31918 is working an up unfitted freight. My notes do not give a time but the slight shadows suggest late morning. I took no other shots that day so maybe I had advance information of this working though it seems that I had seen it before (page 55). By then the W class were mainly working trip freights in the London area. 31918 was withdrawn in August 1963 having been based at Norwood Junction for most of its life. It was built to a Maunsell design at Ashford in June 1935.

The next photo is taken at Riddlesdown Viaduct which at 154 yards long spans a now disused chalk quarry immediately south of the 837 yard long Riddlesdown tunnel. There is a footpath across the line here and I used to cycle there as it was within easy reach of the then quiet A22. My trusty British-made Elswick Lincoln Imp bicycle which took me many a mile can be seen in this picture. The train is the 4.20 pm London Bridge to East Grinstead, a five coach train of mixed Maunsell and Bulleid stock headed by BR class four 2-6-4 tank No. 80085.

The Oxted line then continues hugging the east side of the valley on its way to Upper Warlingham and I managed to find another path crossing which I used a few times. On the same day as the previous shot, Friday 3rd May 1963, BR Standard class four 4-6-0 No. 75069 is on the 3.54 pm Victoria to Brighton and Eastbourne, which will divide at Eridge. The Stewarts Lane based engine was coping well with its eight coach 285 ton train of Bulleid stock and was running exactly on time at 4.20 pm.

At the same location but on the other side of the crossing on the grim cold day of Saturday 10th February 1962, C class 0-6-0 No. 31719 heads an up train of unfitted vans at 11.10 am. This is almost certainly the same train as seen on page 52. This sturdy Wainwright designed engine was built by Sharp Stewart and Co in January 1901 and was withdrawn from Norwood Junction shed in May 1962, just three months after this photo was taken. Sister engine 31592 is preserved on the Bluebell Railway in SECR colours as No. 592.

Upper Warlingham on a very cold and wet 20th September 1961. Schools class 4-4-0 No. 30917 *Ardingly* heads an up six coach train of mixed stock. This is probably the 7.17 am Brighton to London Bridge service. Brighton based 30917 was built at Eastleigh in June 1933 and withdrawn in November 1962. It was one of the class fitted with Lemaitre multiple-jet blast pipes with wide chimney, which improved performance but in my view did not enhance its looks.

Woldingham station on a sunny but cold Saturday, 4th November 1961. BR Standard class four 2-6-4 tank No. 80013 leaving on a down morning train from Victoria to Tunbridge Wells West. I had started the day at East Croydon before moving to Upper Warlingham, Woldingham, East Croydon again, then Norwood Junction shed, West Croydon (page 37) and finally Selsdon, all on my Elswick Lincoln Imp bicycle! 80013 was built at Brighton in 1951 and lasted until June 1966.

The 20th of May 1962 was a Sunday and there were engineering works that day which affected the Croydon area, and up trains were running as far as Sanderstead with the engines running round trains there and returning very quickly. This shot of a down train at 10.30 am was taken at milepost 17½ between Woldingham station and the tunnel and shows BR Standard class four 2-6-4 tank No. 80084 running bunker first due to the procedure of running round its train at Sanderstead.

Half an hour later at 11 am at the same location Standard tank No. 80140 was photographed on an up train on this warm spring day. The driver seemed surprised to see me lurking under the trees. I had no lineside permit so would have been in trouble if reported and caught, though engine crews tended not to take any action in those days. The same engine and train returned half an hour later with 80140 running bunker first. There must have been some slick work by all concerned at Sanderstead that day.

From the one mile 501 yard long tunnel under the North Downs after Woldingham the line drops down to Oxted, which in the spring of 1962 was still busy with steam on the London trains and on the hourly shuttle to Tunbridge Wells West via Edenbridge and Groombridge. BR Standard class four 2-6-4 tank No. 80059 is taking water having arrived on the 2.08 pm from Victoria, which we had travelled on from East Croydon. The engine is in filthy condition though the cab side number has been cleaned.

H class 0-4-4 tank No. 31543, exile from the Westerham branch, (page 10) is waiting in the down bay platform with the 3.04 pm push-pull train to Tunbridge Wells West while 80059 is still taking water on the 2.08 pm from Victoria. It's Saturday 24th March 1962 but the very cold day hasn't deterred a number of enthusiasts from being present. We caught the 4.46 pm train back to East Croydon, hauled by 80010, and in the time at Oxted saw nine different steam locos.

One of the nine was H class 0-4-4 tank, No. 31324. This was another loco which used to work the Westerham branch before it closed on 28th October 1961. It arrived at Oxted at 4.37 pm on the 4 pm from Tunbridge Wells West. Because the train comprised two coaches, one of which is an ex SECR 10 compartment second class coach, and two 4 wheeled utility vans rather than the usual push pull set, the engine had to run round the train and then push it towards London before setting back onto the down line and then into the bay platform to form the 5.04 pm return train. This shot shows the train crossing over from the up to the down line. Though this manoeuvre was undertaken at some speed, it delayed our 4.46 pm back to East Croydon by four minutes.

This shot was taken on the Oxted side of the tunnel which leads to Hurst Green on Saturday, 25th November 1961. It shows H class No. 31543 on a shuttle train from Tunbridge Wells West. I can't recall how I got to the line but I was standing at the end of the viaduct over the A25 road which was far below. 31543 is pulling Set No. 652 which had an ex SECR 10 compartment 3rd coach plus a ex LSWR brake composite fitted for push pull working. On the left are the signals for Hurst Green; the distant signal is for the line to Edenbridge and the signals on the right for East Grinstead.

A week later, Saturday 2nd December 1961 was mild and sunny so we decided to cover the Oxted and Redhill to Tonbridge lines in the Troy Town area, near to Edenbridge. This shot is at Crowhurst Junction on the Redhill to Tonbridge line which connected to the Oxted line enabling trains to transfer between the two when travelling southbound from Oxted or west from Tonbridge. It was last used on 3rd January 1965. BR Standard class four 2-6-4 tank No. 80145 is going very well indeed with an unusually heavy train from Redhill to Tonbridge. What superb and versatile engines these were. This one wasn't built at Brighton until 1956 and withdrawn from Bournemouth shed in June 1967.

The Oxted line passes underneath the Redhill line by means of a double tunnel, emerging into the open after it crosses under the Redhill line. Trains ran from Hurst Green to the next stop at Edenbridge Town, 4.3 miles mainly downhill on gradients as steep as 1-in-103 so speed could be quite high at the southern exit of the tunnel. On the same day as the previous shot, H class 0-4-4 tank No. 31543 is pushing Maunsell Set No. 602 at an estimated 70 mph which would have been pretty exciting on the train, or indeed the footplate!

An hour later H class No. 31005 is pulling Set No. 656 which appears to be made up of a ex LSWR Brake Composite at the camera end plus an ex LSWR brake 3rd. This afternoon train is clearly not travelling as fast as the one in the previous shot. 31005 was the oldest survivor of its class and was built at Ashford in May 1907, lasting until September 1963 being one of the last to be withdrawn.

Up above and a bit further east on the Redhill line, Maunsell U1 class 2-6-0 No. 31899 is seen plodding slowly along with an afternoon train from Tonbridge to Redhill, using the same Maunsell flat sided 'Hastings' stock as in the photo on page 64. The U1s were 3 cylinder versions of the U class and were built at Eastleigh in 1931. It was withdrawn as non standard with most of the U1s in December 1962.

Also at Troy Town but this time on Friday 3rd May 1963 is Ivatt 2-6-2 tank No. 41326 on Set 602 working the 1.04 pm Oxted to Tunbridge Wells West. It was very unusual indeed to see a Brighton based Ivatt tank on these shuttle trains and this is the only time I saw this happening. The other engine on these services that day was H class No. 31518.

After Edenbridge on the Oxted line is Hever then the delightfully situated Cowden. On Saturday 31st March 1962 we undertook an expedition by train to Groombridge. We caught the 8.29 am from East Croydon to Oxted behind BR Standard tank No. 80138 and then transferred to the 9.04 am Tunbridge Wells train as far as Cowden, hauled by H class 0-4-4 tank No. 31324 which is seen here at Cowden sitting in the bright spring sunshine. After an hour we caught the next down train at 10.24 am behind H class No. 31278.

Groombridge was an absolute delight and very busy with all trains steam hauled in 1962 and 1963. As well as the hourly push-pull trains to and from Tunbridge Wells and Oxted there were the hourly London trains to and from Tunbridge Wells via East Grinstead and hourly trains from Tonbridge to Brighton and from Tunbridge Wells to Eastbourne, both via Eridge. This gave a total of eight trains an hour altogether; a veritable steam paradise. No wonder it was much visited. We walked to the junction of the lines to East Grinstead and Oxted with those to Eridge situated in an idyllic location from where good photos could be had in all directions. H class No. 31278 is taking the line to Oxted via the Ashurst loop on the 11 am from Tunbridge Wells.

At the station, BR standard class four 2-6-4 tank No. 80094 is entering with the 11.47 am train from Tunbridge Wells West to Victoria, comprised mainly of Bulleid stock. The station still exists today though in much reduced form on the Spa Valley heritage line.

The rest of that day, 31st March 1962, was spent at the junction and on the line towards East Grinstead near Ashurst Junction. It's here that BR Standard class four 2-6-4 tank No. 80010 is seen crossing the road from Groombridge to Crowborough on an afternoon train to Victoria. Back at Groombridge station we caught the 2.53 pm to Oxted via East Grinstead hauled by No. 80094 and after more photography returned to East Croydon on the 4.46 pm train behind BR Standard tank No. 80038.

Two weeks before our visit to Groombridge we were on our bikes for another long day, this time starting at Tonbridge. On Saturday 17th March 1962 BR Standard class four 2-6-4 tank No. 80032 is storming the 1-in-53 climb out of Tonbridge towards Somerhill tunnel with the 11.10 am train to Brighton via Tunbridge Wells West and Eridge. Over the years I have spent many hours on the footbridge from where this shot was taken, including photographing and tape recording the Hastings diesels on their last day of operation in May 1986.

The lure of Groombridge was too much to resist on Saturday 17th March 1962 and so here we see BR Standard tank No. 80144 leaving on the 12.10 pm Tonbridge to Brighton with a four coach train of mixed Maunsell and Bulleid coaching stock. It's another beautiful but cold spring day and there is little sign that winter is nearly finished.

At the junction the sun is perfect for this shot of H class 0-4-4 tank No. 31522 heading the 1 pm Tunbridge Wells West to Oxted. The push pull set is probably Set 652 as the first coach is an ex SECR 10 compartment 3rd. I didn't see No. 31522 working very often but the other engine on the shuttles was one of the regulars, No. 31278. 31522 was built at Ashford in August 1909 and withdrawn in January 1963. It was based at Tunbridge Wells shed.

While the Standard tanks predominated on the London, Brighton and Eastbourne services, Maunsell's Moguls did appear on a fairly regular basis. Here N class 2-6-0 No. 31871 is on the 2.10 pm Tonbridge to Brighton with Maunsell four coach set 451 at Groombridge Junction also on Saturday, 17th March 1962. The engine was built at Ashford in 1925. It was shedded at Redhill so presumably got to Tonbridge on a freight or maybe passenger working.

It's now the damp summer of 1962 and on Saturday 2nd June I spent some time east of Groombridge, near High Rocks. BR Standard class four 2-6-4 tank No. 80019 is running bunker first on set 779 working the 8.43 am Eastbourne to Tunbridge Wells West. It is passing the 10 am Tunbridge Wells to Oxted which had H class No. 31533 on push pull set 606. Set 779 was one of 31 such three coach Bulleid sets used extensively on the Southern at that time.

Facing south at Groombridge Junction towards Eridge on the same day another bunker first BR Standard tank, this one No. 80145, is heading the 9.45 am Eastbourne to Tonbridge. This section of line is still open, run by The Spa Valley Railway.

Another line which received a lot of attention was the branch from Three Bridges to East Grinstead. In 1962 and 1963 it was worked by M7 and H class 0-4-4 tanks with push pull sets and ran through lovely scenery, with many places to photograph the trains. On Sunday 15th April 1962, M7 tank No. 30055 is heading Maunsell push pull set 619 on the 12.08 pm from Three Bridges on the climb soon after leaving that station.

No. 30055 again, this time on Sunday 19th May 1963, pausing at Grange Road with the 1.40 pm from East Grinstead to Three Bridges. Although the hourly service over the seven mile line could be worked easily by one engine and push pull set, it was the practice to change sets at lunchtime, maybe for engine crew purposes. The morning trains had been worked by H class No. 31518. Drummond-designed 30055 was built at Nine Elms works in 1905 and was based at Three Bridges.

At the same location on Sunday 26th May 1963, the now preserved H class 0-4-4 tank No. 31263 is running in with the 12.40 pm from East Grinstead to Three Bridges. Grange Road station was opened in 1860 and closed with the line in January 1967. Nothing remains as shops and housing cover the site.

Earlier on that very hot Sunday morning, No.31263 is storming up the 1-in-88 climb out of Three Bridges with the 11.08 am to East Grinstead. It will soon arrive at Rowfant station, built to serve the estate of Curtis Lampson, and was opened in 1855.

The afternoon service on 26th May 1963 was worked by H class No. 31518 and this shot was taken at the remote and little used Rowfant station. The train is the 3.08 pm from Three Bridges which has just drawn to an abrupt halt causing water from the tank to overflow. The train would continue up a 1-in-80 climb to Grange Road station.

I rarely ventured south to Brighton but managed to get this shot of E4 class 0-6-2 tank No. 32474 sitting in the centre road there on 26th July 1962. Also noted that day at Brighton were Bulleid rebuilt West Country class pacific No. 34014 *Budleigh Salterton* and ex LBSCR Terrier No.32670. In the background of this shot is one of the Bulleid 4 Lav units, either 2954 or 2955.

The remaining four photos on steam on the Central Division are all of an extraordinary railtour named 'The Sussex Coast Limited' which took place on Sunday 24th June 1962. It started at London Waterloo behind preserved T9 class 4-4-0 No. 120 (30120), built in 1899. It went via Cobham to Guildford and Horsham, with a photo stop at Cranleigh. At Horsham the T9 gave way to E4 class 0-6-2 tank No. 32503 built in 1900 and E6 class 0-6-2 tank built in 1905. Here is the pair of them on the seven coach special at Horsham.

The special then proceeded to Midhurst via Pulborough with a photo stop at Selham. We reversed at Midhurst from 12.52 pm to 1.17 pm and the two locos can be seen here running round their train on what was now a very hot day. By the time of our visit the Midhurst line had been reduced to freight only status (in 1955) and would close finally in 1966.

From Midhurst the two Brighton tanks took us back to Pulborough on the Arun Valley line and here we reversed again to be taken on to Bognor Regis by K class 2-6-0 No. 32353. This Billington designed engine was built as late as 1921 and was withdrawn at the end of 1962. It is seen here reversing out of the station amongst the semaphore signals in order to turn and take the train forward to Haywards Heath at just before 3 pm. On the left is a 4 Cor unit.

At Haywards Heath the T9 joined us again and took the train on to Eastbourne via Lewes. After a final reversal the T9 headed back to London Bridge via Heathfield, Eridge, East Grinstead and East Croydon. There was a pilot engine as far as Rotherfield in the form of M7 class No. 30055 and I can still clearly remember the racket from the two engines as they climbed the steep gradients of the Cuckoo line. This shot is taken at Rotherfield after the M7 had been removed. We arrived back at London Bridge just 13 minutes late after a wonderful day out during which we had travelled 233 miles behind five different locos.

South Western Lines

Moving on to the South Western Division, photos are set out in roughly geographic order from London, starting at Waterloo. I spent many hours here watching and photographing trains in the 1960s steam era and later and I worked there in 1966 and in the early 1970s. On Sunday 10th September 1961 rebuilt Merchant Navy class pacific No. 35017 *Belgian Marine* is preparing to leave on the 9 am train to Plymouth and Torrington.

A busy scene at Waterloo on Saturday, 23rd May 1964. Rebuilt West Country class 4-6-2 No 34108 *Wincanton* is waiting on the nine coach 9.30 am to Bournemouth. This was a semi fast train calling at Surbiton, Woking, Basingstoke, Winchester, Eastleigh, Southampton Central, Brockenhurst and Bournemouth Central, arriving at the West at 12.38 pm. On the right is BR Standard class five 4-6-0 No. 73112 *Morgan Le Fay* on the five coach 9.54 am stopping train to Basingstoke, fast to Woking, and in the bay on the left is a BR Standard class three 2-6-2 tank on empty stock duties. I travelled on the 9.54 am train, and the BR Five produced the usual solid performance to keep time with a maximum speed of 70 mph.

This classic scene at Vauxhall is probably my all time favourite steam photo. On Tuesday 17th May 1966 rebuilt Merchant Navy class pacific No. 35008 *Orient Line* is just getting under way with Nine Elms Duty 434, the 12.30 pm Waterloo to Bournemouth 'Bournemouth Belle'. The train consists of 11 Pullman coaches and a bogie van which would weigh about 500 tons full. The pose of the Nine Elms driver suggests that he is just winding the cut off lever back having got speed up to about 30 mph. 35008 lasted until the end of Southern steam in July 1967 and was one of the 100 mph engines, reaching 102 mph down Grateley bank on 5th July of that year.

Friday, 29th September 1961, was a fine autumn day so I caught the number 54 bus to East Croydon and a Southern electric to Clapham Junction where I spent the next few hours watching and photographing trains. Here we see M7 class 0-4-4 tank No. 30245 shunting some Bulleid empty stock apparently on Nine Elms Duty 7. Drummond 30245, classified 2P, was built at Nine Elms works in April 1897 and withdrawn in November 1962. It is preserved as part of the National collection at York.

A few minutes later, BR Standard class five 4-6-0 No. 73115 passed slowly through on an up freight working. It is about to pass M7 tank No. 30039 on an empty stock working, possibly from the 9.33 am arrival at Waterloo from Bournemouth West. It is running underneath Clapham Junction A Box. This is the signal box which collapsed in May 1965 and subsequently has its cladding removed. 73115 had taken the name of *King Pellinore* from N15 class No. 30738, withdrawn in 1958. 30039 was withdrawn in May 1963.

The platforms are remarkably empty as clean rebuilt Merchant Navy class 4-6-2 No. 35017 *Belgian Marine* passes on time with the 10.30 am Waterloo to Weymouth. This was a Nine Elms top link turn and was fast to Southampton Central and Bournemouth in just two hours for the 108 miles, the front portion reaching Weymouth in exactly three hours. After this train had passed GWR class 5700 0-6-0 Pannier Tank No. 9770 appeared in the yard. These engines shared the empty stock work with the LSWR Drummond M7s from 1959 until the end of 1962/ early 1963. The GWR engines were not liked by the Nine Elms crews.

At 10.41 am, rebuilt West Country class 4-6-2 No. 34031 *Torrington* passed on an up Ocean Liner Express from Southampton Docks carrying a headboard proclaiming 'Holland America Line'. This was followed by the up 'Royal Wessex' headed by No. 35024 *East Asiatic Company* running exactly on time at 10.43 am. Then with the platforms still empty the legendary 'Atlantic Coast Express' appeared, seen here with Rebuilt Merchant Navy pacific No. 35029 *Ellerman Lines* on 12 coaches. This train was only allowed 80 minutes for the 83.7 miles to Salisbury and reached Exeter in two minutes under three hours. Standing in the yard is No. 35020 *Bibby Line* which had earlier arrived at Waterloo on the 9.33 am.

The next location is Clapham cutting where this shot was taken on Sunday, 23rd June 1963. Passengers on the 9.20 am Excursion from Waterloo to Bournemouth had the unexpected pleasure of super power in the form Bulleid rebuilt Merchant Navy class pacific No. 35023 *Holland Afrika Line*. This was closely followed by the 9.23 am Excursion from Waterloo to Salisbury, worked by No. 34031 *Torrington*. 35023 was another of the 100 mph Bulleids, possibly the best known one, with Bert Hooker driving at Andover on 15th October 1966. On 23rd June 1963, LM Black 5s Nos. 44844 and 44870 were photographed on through trains from the Midlands to the South coast on the Central Division metals.

Facing the other way from the same bridge on 23rd June 1963, this shot shows rebuilt Merchant Navy pacific No. 35022 *Holland America Line* on the 7.17 am from Yeovil Town to Waterloo, due at 11.02 am. This interesting train reversed at Yeovil Junction, then called at all stations to Salisbury except Milborne Port. It was then fast to Andover Junction and Basingstoke and all stations to Woking. Here it left at 10.28 am taking the up slow line to be overtaken by an up Portsmouth electric which left at the same time on the fast line. 35022 would then have crossed over to the fast line at Hampton Court Junction to run up to Waterloo behind the Portsmouth train.

Further down Clapham cutting good photos could be taken from the last overbridge carrying Heathfield Road. LN class 4-6-0 No. 30861 *Lord Anson* is heading a down empty stock train to Basingstoke under the busy A214 Trinity Road bridge at 2.10 pm on 16th June 1962. I visited this location a lot by bicycle from my home in Shirley, near Croydon. 1962 was the last year when the older loco classes could be seen. On that afternoon, amongst the Bulleid pacifics and BR Standards, I photographed LN class Nos. 30857, 30861 and 30862 plus Schools No. 30902. I had no advance information on these, so serendipity indeed.

Facing the other way on the hot evening of 31st May 1963 this shot shows rebuilt Merchant Navy class pacific No. 35005 *Canadian Pacific* on the up 'Bournemouth Belle', running a few minutes late. 35005 is a record breaking engine, holding the blue ribbon for the fastest time with steam from Waterloo to Basingstoke on 15th May 1965 in the hands of driver Gordon Hooper. On the same evening it also reached 105 mph down Roundwood bank with the same driver in charge. It is preserved on the Mid Hants railway after a spell on the main line and is now being overhauled for further service, though not unfortunately on the main line.

Durnsford Road, about six miles from Waterloo, was the location of a power station and also carriage sidings for electric stock. One of my most photographed trains was the 8.46 am Salisbury to Waterloo due at 11.16 am. It featured a lot because in 1961 and 1962 it was a regular turn for Salisbury-based N15 King Arthur class 4-6-0, and No. 30451 *Sir Lamorak* was the engine which seemed to dominate. This photo was taken of it passing the Railway Staff Halt on Friday, 22nd September 1961. On the left the up slow line can be seen descending from the Wimbledon Flyover and on the right is a 12 coach train of Portsmouth electric stock.

Wimbledon, 7.2 miles from Waterloo, was another much visited location as it had two footbridges and a footpath to the west of the station and was within easy cycling distance. N15 class 4-6-0 No. 30451 *Sir Lamorak* is seen again on the 8.46 am Salisbury to Waterloo approaching the station on Monday, 18th September 1961. The engine worked back to Salisbury on the 2.54 pm semi fast service so I must have spent the day there as I also photographed this at Wimbledon. The reliability of this engine was quite extraordinary as it continued to work this turn on frequent occasions until at least the end of April 1962. It was withdrawn in June that year.

Taken from the furthest footbridge, BR Standard class five 4-6-0 No. 73089 *Maid of Astolat* is in charge of a train of Bulleid stock on the 9.30 am Waterloo to Bournemouth West on Saturday 4th May 1963. 73089 was then based at Nine Elms having been a Stewarts Lane engine from new until the completion of Kent Coast electrification in 1959. I travelled just 73 miles behind it, though 73089 lasted nearly to the end of steam being withdrawn in June 1967.

On summer Saturdays in 1962 the Lymington Pier boat trains were the preserve of the Schools class 4-4-0s due to the restricted length of the turntable at Brockenhurst. At the same location as the previous shot on Saturday 25th August 1962 No. 30902 *Wellington* makes a fine sight on the 8.45 am Waterloo to Lymington Pier. The train was booked to pick up passengers at Winchester and then called at Southampton Central and Brockenhurst. There were three such trains each way and on that day the 9.42 am down was hauled by No. 30935 *Sevenoaks* and the 12 noon train by 30936 *Cranleigh*.

While the Schools class engines almost always worked the down trains, substitutions on the up trains were quite common. This shot shows LN class 4-6-0 No. 30861 *Lord Anson* on the 3.30 pm Lymington Pier to Waterloo approaching Wimbledon on Saturday, 9th September 1961. The train was running some minutes early which suggests that this replacement loco was found in good time and that the planned engine didn't fail en route. 30861 was one of the last of its class to be withdrawn in October 1962. On the left of the picture is the line from Sutton, still semaphore signalled on that date.

This location by the footbridge near to Wimbledon 'C' signal box was one of my favourites to photograph the procession of weekday evening trains and I spent many an evening there after work when the daylight allowed. One train which was always of interest was the 7.02 pm Parcels from Waterloo to Bournemouth. This train was normally a Feltham S15 class 4-6-0 and this shot taken on Wednesday 23rd May 1962 shows Urie S15 class 4-6-0 No. 30511. The 7.40 pm which followed was booked for an Eastleigh LN class 4-6-0 and on that evening it was No. 30850 *Lord Nelson*. 30511 was built at Eastleigh in 1921 and lasted until July 1963. No less than seven of the class have been preserved.

Just beyond Raynes Park station in the early 1960s was a meadow next to Carters Seeds and in the shadow of the bridge carrying the Kingston bypass over the railway. This was a pleasant spot to watch trains and here we see rebuilt Merchant Navy class pacific No. 35030 *Elder Dempster Lines* on the 11 am Atlantic Coast Express from Waterloo to points west. The date is Saturday 8th June 1963, which was a week before the summer timetable started. 35030 had the honour of working the last steam hauled train into Waterloo, the 2.11 pm from Weymouth on Sunday, 9th July 1967. I travelled 1,634 miles behind it between 1962 and 1967.

Another much visited location was New Malden, 8.6 miles from Waterloo. A track crossed the line on the London side of the station and it's still a good spot today. On a benign autumn day, Sunday 3rd November 1963, rebuilt Merchant Navy class pacific No. 35020 *Bibby Line* heads the lightly loaded 10.30 am Waterloo to Bournemouth and Weymouth, first stop Winchester. This train was usually 10 or 11 coaches, and the eight coaches on this day looks like a scratch set, with a Bulleid brake second leading.

As an evening location New Malden was second only to Wimbledon and I somehow managed to get access to the lineside to make maximum use of the beautiful evening light for this shot of rebuilt West Country class 4-6-2 No. 34028 *Eddystone* taken on Friday, 17th May 1963. The train is the 4.05 pm Salisbury to Waterloo which was due to arrive at 7.08 pm having taken over three hours for its journey of 83.7 miles. It called at all stations to Woking, then Weybridge and Surbiton. 34028 was withdrawn in May 1964 and is preserved on the Swanage Railway.

The evening before, Thursday, 16th May 1963, I managed to get this photograph of a Rebuilt light pacific on the up 'Bournemouth Belle', booked for Merchant Navy pacific. No. 34044 *Woolacombe* was a Bournemouth based engine with a reputation for good performances so it would have had little trouble handling this 455 ton train on its pre two hour schedule. It was the last of the Bournemouth fast trains to be given a two hour schedule which it was with the summer 1963 timetable from 17th June.

Sunday, 2nd December 1962, saw a very unusual railtour run on South Western metals in the London area. This involved two of the Beattie 2-4-0 well tanks No. 30585 and 30587, both built in 1874, plus H15 class 4-6-0 tank No. 30517. The route was Waterloo–East Putney–Hampton Court–Wimbledon Yard–Chessington South–Wimbledon Yard–Shepperton–Richmond–Waterloo. Passing New Malden returning from Hampton Court are the two tank engines with their six coach train. The tour was repeated on 16th December, after which the two Beatties were withdrawn. Both engines are preserved, 30585 by the Quainton Railway Society and 30587 by the NRM but located at the Bodmin and Wenford Railway.

Coal was still big business for the railways in the 1960s. Walton-on-Thames along with many other stations had a small yard where coal was delivered by rail to the local coal merchant. On the misty morning of Saturday 27th April 1963 Q1 class 0-6-0 No. 33001 is shunting the yard. Forty of these powerful ugly duckling freight locos were built to a design by Oliver Bulleid at Ashford and Brighton in 1942 to meet wartime requirements. 33001 was withdrawn in May 1964 but is preserved in the National collection at York. On the main line the up fast line home signal is pulled off for West Country class pacific No. 34003 *Plymouth* on the 6.45 am Salisbury to Waterloo.

On the same day about forty minutes later the Q1 has finished its shunting and gone and two rebuilt Merchant Navy pacifics, 35004 and 35021, have passed by before rebuilt Battle of Britain class 4-6-2 No. 34082 *615 Squadron* appeared on the 9.30 am Waterloo to Bournemouth West. The Nine Elms driver is looking composed and should have few worries working this light eight coach train of Bulleid stock running nicely on time after the Surbiton stop.

Weybridge, 19.1 miles from Waterloo, was a good place to photograph trains, especially before the fine array of semaphore signals were swept away. This scene is redolent of the classic railway with a steam hauled train, a busy goods shed and a beautiful signal gantry. The date is Saturday 16th May 1964, which was part of a bank holiday weekend and the train is the 8.46 am Salisbury to Waterloo previously the regular 'King Arthur' turn seen on pages 100 and 101. By 1964 it was a Salisbury Bulleid pacific duty and on that day it was rebuilt West Country No. 34014 *Budleigh Salterton*.

By 30th April 1966 the semaphore signals had gone but these two Maunsell Moguls still make a fine sight storming past on the 9.59 am from Waterloo RCTS special train to the Longmoor Military Railway. The lead engine is U class No. 31791 and the train engine U class No. 31639. These were the last two of Richard Maunsell's fine design and were both withdrawn in June that year. The lady on the right is about to board the 9.57 am Waterloo to Alton electric train comprised of 2 Bil stock. In the station approach road a London Transport RF bus waits for passengers.

Just west of Weybridge station a track crossed the lines on an overbridge and made a good vantage point. Facing towards Woking another set of semaphore signals could be used to frame up trains, as here on Saturday 22nd June 1963 with Battle of Britain pacific No. 34092 *City of Wells* on Salisbury Duty 491, the 12 noon Ilfracombe to Waterloo. It's early in the season which accounts for the lightly loaded eight coach train which ran fast from Exeter Central to Salisbury and then nonstop to Waterloo with Nine Elms men. 34092 is preserved on the East Lancs Railway and has had spells on the main line producing some very high speed runs in the process.

It's that engine again on the 8.46 am Salisbury to Waterloo, this time at Woking on Saturday 28th April 1962. Such was the consistency of its appearance that a small group of us was able to plan in advance a one day rover ticket to include a run behind it. 1925 built N15 class 4-6-0 No. 30451 *Sir Lamorak* is seen here entering Woking on the up slow line. Driver Cambray of Salisbury shed took us up to Waterloo in fine style with a maximum speed of 76 mph. Its diagram was worked by a Bulleid pacific from June 1962, when 30451 was withdrawn.

Woking, 24.3 miles from Waterloo, is the junction of the Portsmouth and West of England main lines and it was a good place to linger to see steam hauled trains to and from the west passing at high speed. The date is Saturday 11th April 1964 and Eastleigh based rebuilt West Country class pacific No. 34004 *Yeovil* is running very fast with an up Ocean Liner Express from Southampton Docks to Waterloo. The fireman is taking a breather with the hard work now all done. The train is watched by quite a few fellow enthusiasts and at least one duffle bag can be seen, no doubt containing a bottle of Tizer for it was a hot day, in complete contrast to the Saturday before when it had been snowing!

As late as summer Saturdays in 1963 Feltham based S15 class 4-6-0s had a regular passenger turn on the 3.54 pm Waterloo to Basingstoke semi fast service. Here No. 30829 is approaching its first stop at Woking on 29th June 1963. They could be quite speedy and generally had no trouble keeping time. 30829 was built in 1927 to Maunsell's design which was a development of the original design by Urie. The batch from 30823 to 30832 had a higher boiler pressure and eight-wheeled tenders. 30829 was withdrawn in November 1963.

West of Woking is a footbridge which spans both the Portsmouth and west of England lines. On a fine and warm Bank Holiday Monday, 3rd June 1963, rebuilt Merchant Navy class pacific No. 35030 *Elder Dempster Lines* is making good progress with the heavy 8.15 am Waterloo to Weymouth Quay 'Channel Islands Express'. On arrival at Weymouth Quay at 11.46 am passengers would transfer to the steamer, probably *Caesarea* or *Sarnia*, for Guernsey where arrival was at 4.30 pm or Jersey at 7 pm. The second class single fare in 1963 was 4 pounds 18 shillings and 3 pence.

Approaching Woking on the line from Guildford and Portsmouth at 7.10 am on Saturday 1st June 1963 is a freight train from Redhill headed by S15 class 4-6-0 No. 30847. It was the last of its class built in 1936 at Eastleigh and was withdrawn in January 1964. It is preserved on the Bluebell Railway. For the last few months of its life on the main line it was shedded at Redhill where it was fitted with a smaller six wheel tender to fit the turntable there.

As noted earlier in this book, the up Lymington Pier trains sometimes had the booked Schools class 4-4-0 substituted. This was the last year in service for the class and some of them had become very run down. Here on Saturday 18th August 1962, N15 class 4-6-0 No. 30765 *Sir Gareth* on the 1.28 pm Lymington Pier to Waterloo is a very unusual replacement for No. 30937 *Epsom* which had worked the 9.42 am train down from Waterloo. Locos were detached and attached at Brockenhurst where they had to be turned and serviced in quite a short time. 30902 *Wellington* had worked down on the 8.45 am train and returned as booked on the 11.43 up train. This shot was taken about two miles west of Woking at Hook Heath where a footbridge crossed the line. 30765 was running late and travelling very fast, suggesting a late substitution.

The next shots are taken further down the line just beyond Pirbright Junction where the Alton line diverged. On what was now the very hot day of Saturday 1st June 1963 BR Standard class 9F 2-10-0 No.92211 appeared at 11.15 am on heavy freight train on the down slow line. It wasn't unusual to see this class on freights in 1963 as five of the class were allocated to Eastleigh for a short time. 92211 had an incredibly short life as it emerged from Swindon works in September 1959 and was withdrawn in May 1967, less than eight years later. What a waste of a superb resource.

At the same spot on the same day, rebuilt Merchant Navy class pacific No. 35002 *Union Castle* is storming the 1-in-298 gradient to Milepost 31 just over a mile away. The train is the heavy 11.05 am 'Atlantic Coast Express' relief from Waterloo shown as SPL 10. This was because the 1st of June was prior to the start of the summer timetable on 17th June but extra untimetabled trains were running as it was a Bank Holiday weekend. The three coach Bulleid set at the front of the train plus maybe the next two coaches were probably bound for Plymouth while the remainder of the train would have been for Bude and Padstow. At various locations on that beautiful summer day I took 42 photos of steam hauled trains, forgoing many more opportunities.

On Saturday 4th August 1962 Bulleid Battle of Britain class pacific No. 34064 *Fighter Command* has just topped the summit of the climb from West Byfleet at Milepost 31 with the 10.54 am Waterloo to Swanage. This train called only at Southampton Central, Wareham and Corfe Castle before arriving at Swanage at 2.10 pm. 34064 was fitted with a Giesel ejector which was designed to improve draughting and reduce coal consumption. The late Gordon Hooper, who was one of the top drivers at Nine Elms, always reckoned that 34064 was nearly as good as one the bigger Merchant Navy pacifics.

Farnborough, 33.2 miles from Waterloo, had a superb set of ex LSWR pneumatically controlled lower quadrant signals which were a feature of the line between Woking and Basingstoke. These were introduced in 1902 and lasted until resignalling in 1966. They were worked by low pressure air at 15 psi and if you were close enough you could hear the hiss as the signal was changed. On Saturday 21st July 1962 I had arrived at Farnborough behind No. 34062 *17 Squadron* on the 7.22 am from Waterloo to break my journey on the way to Basingstoke and Worting Junction. At 8.30 am S15 No. 30507 passed on a freight seen here on the up slow line. After that I photographed No. 30925 *Cheltenham* on the 8.24 am Basingstoke to Waterloo local and No.34071 *601 Squadron* on the down Channel Islands Boat train. I then caught the 9.07 am local behind No. 30857 *Lord Howe*. What amazing variety in just over 40 minutes!

To continue the story of that summer Saturday, 21st July 1962, I have moved to Worting Junction, 50.3 miles from Waterloo, for the next two shots. This busy scene shows two BR Standard class five 4-6-0s. On the left is No. 73089 on the 9.35 am Waterloo to Bournemouth West on the fast line passing No. 73047 on the 9.25 am Wimbledon to Weymouth. The 9.35 am was fast to Southampton Central in 102 minutes for the 79.3 miles and the Wimbledon train made calls at Surbiton, Woking and Farnborough before reaching Basingstoke.

The next photo shows the late running 9.42 am Waterloo to Lymington Pier train headed by Schools class 4-4-0 No. 30934 *St Lawrence*. This was behind No. 73139 on the 8.43 am Wolverhampton Low level to Portsmouth Harbour and No. 34061 on the 10.05 am Waterloo to Bournemouth West. The reason for the lateness was that Nine Elms driver Bert Fordrey had failed No. 30936 *Cranleigh* at Basingstoke and taken 30934 in its place. He set about recovering lost time, getting the train up to 80 mph down Roundwood bank. The 21st of July was a very busy day even by summer Saturday standards as there were also some Ocean Liner Expresses running. I took 61 photos of steam hauled trains, the most in one day in the days of steam.

At the end of the day I walked the three miles back to Basingstoke to wait for a suitable train to London. I was fortunate that soon N15 class 4-6-0 No. 30793 *Sir Ontzlake* appeared on the 5.15 pm stopping train from Salisbury and so after photographing its arrival I caught it. I timed the run throughout by stopwatch though nothing special was needed to keep time, just a maximum speed of 64 mph at Hersham. 30793 was introduced in 1926 for Central Division services and withdrawn just one month after my run behind it.

At Basingstoke again, now on Wednesday 20th April 1966, this is the sight which often greeted us after we had alighted from a steam hauled run down from Waterloo. The fireman is checking the results of his efforts while Nine Elms driver Ted Male is taking a breather on rebuilt Battle of Britain class pacific No. 34056 *Croydon*. The train is the 6 pm from Waterloo to Salisbury which the driver had brought down from Waterloo in just over 61 minutes, arriving two minutes early. Standing on the down slow line is a BR Standard class 5 on the 5.43 pm semi fast train from Waterloo.

By 11th December 1965 when this photo was taken at Basingstoke, very few of Maunsell's Moguls were left in service. This freight train, worked by N class No. 31809, may have been its last turn as it was withdrawn in January 1966 after a life of over 32 years. These versatile engines also worked passenger trains and had a booked turn on the 6.51 pm Bournemouth to Woking stopping train until June 1965. They also turned up from time to time on the 7.54 pm Waterloo to Basingstoke stopping service which was fast to Woking. I travelled behind N class No. 31873 on this train on Wednesday 19th May 1965 when it just kept time on the 31 minute schedule with a maximum speed of 63 mph. Nine Elms driver Godden was in charge that evening.

Apart from Basingstoke and Worting Junction I did very little photography over the next 25 or so miles to Southampton and any done there tended to be off the down main platform end after the train I had been travelling on had arrived. There is little to suggest that this shot taken on Saturday 13th May 1967 was close to the end of steam. Bulleid rebuilt West Country class pacific No. 34021 *Dartmoor* has lost its nameplates but the semaphore signals are still there and the billy can is resting on the fall plate ready for another cuppa for the engine crew. The train is the 8.35 am from Waterloo to Bournemouth and the driver was Nine Elms veteran Earnie Harvey. 34021 had kept time easily with its 11 coach train, running at 75 mph down Roundwood bank.

Almost the full array of Southampton down starting signals is shown in this photo taken at 4 pm on Sunday 30th June 1963. U class 2-6-0 No. 31613 is working a freight on the up slow line. I was on a Southern Region weekly rail rover and had arrived from Waterloo on the 2.30 pm down summer only train behind No. 34101 *Hartland*. My next train would be the late running 'Pines Express' which had No. 34105 *Swanage* at its head. 34105 is preserved on the Mid Hants Railway.

132 • Southern Steam Recollections

There were very few steam hauled trains on the line to Portsmouth via Guildford and those that there were ran at night or on Sunday diversions so I have none worthy of inclusion in this book. I did however get to Havant a couple of times to cover the line to Hayling Island worked by the charming little Stroudley Terrier 0-6-0 tanks. On Saturday 30th June 1963 No. 32650 is seen here leaving Havant on the 4.05 pm to Hayling Island. 32650 was built in 1876 as LBSCR No. 50 *Whitechapel* and worked on the Isle of Wight as No. W9 *Fishbourne* from 1930 to 1937 before returning to the mainland as Lancing Works shunter. It finally became 32650 in 1953 and was withdrawn in November 1963 when the Hayling Island line closed. It is one of eight Terriers preserved; 32650 is at the Spa Valley Railway as *Sutton*.

At weekends in the summer of 1962 the Hayling Island branch was very busy and ran a half hourly service in each direction. This required three Terrier tanks and in this scene at the terminus on Sunday 29th July 1962 No. 32650 is arriving at 10.45 am on the 10.35 am from Havant while the driver of bunker first No. 32678 is waiting at the end of the platform for the single line token so he could leave with the 10.47 am to Havant. We caught this train to North Hayling for some lineside photography. This intensive service required very slick work by all concerned but the little tanks were up to the job of course. No. 32646 was the other engine that day. 32678 is preserved on the Kent and East Sussex Railway and 32646 is on the Isle of Wight Steam Railway as W8 *Freshwater*.

After returning to Havant behind No. 32650, our little group then caught the train at 12.10 pm to Portsmouth Harbour and the 12.35 pm ferry to Ryde Pier Head. Here O2 class 0-4-4 tank No. 30 awaited us on the 1.28 pm to Ventnor, where the engine is seen about to take water. This cramped little station provided us with some good photo opportunities before we caught the 2.40 pm return train behind No. 35. Twenty-three of this very successful class of Adams tanks worked on the Isle of Wight, officially numbered within the series W1 to W36. They were fitted with Westinghouse air brakes. Steam finished on the Island lines in December 1966 but W24 *Calbourne* is preserved on the Isle of Wight Steam Railway.

Back on the mainland we continue our photographic journey west with this shot taken at Millbrook, the first station beyond Southampton, Good Friday, 27th March 1964. Rebuilt Battle of Britain class pacific No. 34060 *25 Squadron* is working the heavy 12 coach 10.35 am relief train from Waterloo to Bournemouth. The train is made up of mainly Bulleid stock, five coach set No. 836 leading. I had arrived at Southampton on the 9.33 am Excursion from Waterloo which was hauled by Bulleid rebuilt Battle of Britain class pacific No. 34050 *Royal Observer Corps*. It was quite a decent run down with an on time arrival after regaining time lost to Woking with 84 mph at Wallers Ash box.

I spent the day walking to the footbridge beyond Totton station about four miles from Southampton and lingered by the causeway near Redbridge to see the down 'Bournemouth Belle' seen in this shot. Merchant Navy pacific No. 35024 *East Asiatic Company* has the winter load of nine Pullmans and a bogie van to contend with, still around 420 tons in all, but this should prove not to be a problem for the Bulleid. In all on that cold Good Friday I took 16 photos and had to wait in the dark for the return Excursion at 8.44 pm as special fares applied.

Moving on now to Brockenhurst, 92¾ miles from Waterloo; this is the junction for the branch to Lymington Pier and the ferry to Yarmouth Slipway, Isle of Wight. On Friday 20th July 1962 I arrived at Brockenhurst at 8.16 am on the 5.40 am from Waterloo, hauled by rebuilt Battle of Britain class pacific No. 34087 *145 Squadron*. Sitting in the branch platform is M7 class 0-4-4 tank No. 30053 with the 8.41 am to Lymington Pier. The station porters can be seen still sorting the large amount of mail which they had unloaded from the 5.40 am train. 30053 was built at Nine Elms works in 1905, was withdrawn in May 1964 and is preserved on the Swanage Railway.

Bournemouth Central is 108 miles from Waterloo and here the shed was opposite the long down platform. In the days of steam there was always something of interest to see, and here Bulleid pacific No. 34041 *Wilton* in original condition is caught by the evening sun as it rests between duties at 6.35 pm on Wednesday, 3rd July 1963. 34041 entered service in September 1946, numbered 21C141, and was withdrawn on 23rd January 1966. It was Bournemouth based at the time this shot was taken.

A few minutes later BR Standard class four 4-6-0 No. 75079 arrived from Bournemouth West running past the shed with the 6.50 pm local service to Woking. At that time this train was allocated this class of locomotive but changed to a Maunsell Mogul in 1964 and '65, before reverting to BR Standard class four haulage, though more often than not it was a 2-6-0 rather than a 4-6-0. 75079 was built at Swindon in 1956 and withdrawn in November 1966. It is preserved on the Mid Hants Railway.

Drummond M7 class 0-4-4 tank No. 30108 is on shed at Bournemouth on Monday 16th July 1962, looking quite smart. In 1962 the M7s were very busy in the Bournemouth area working empty stock, the Bournemouth West portions of trains plus the Swanage and Lymington branches. I was on a Southern weekly rail rover and had travelled down from Waterloo on the 2.30 pm summer only two hour train behind No. 35020 *Bibby Line*. This fast schedule didn't trouble the big pacific and its light 8 coach train. We had arrived on time after touching 90 mph down the bank after Hinton Admiral. 30108 was built in 1904 as one of the class fitted for push pull working and lasted sixty years in service.

The overall roof at Bournemouth shows well in this shot of rebuilt West Country class 4-6-2 No. 34098 *Templecombe* on a lowly freight turn at 12.10 pm on Sunday, 30th June 1963. 34098 was regarded as being a very fine locomotive in the 1960s and I travelled 868 miles behind it before it was withdrawn near to the end of steam in June 1967. On 17th January 1967 Gordon Porter and Tom Moult were in charge of 34098 when it gave me 95 mph just after Woking while working the 8.51 pm arrival at Waterloo, the famous 'Club Train'. This was my highest speed at that point and the net time of 72 minutes from Southampton to Waterloo was faster than the schedules of today's electrics.

Wareham, at 121 miles from Waterloo, was the station for the branch to Swanage and in 1962 was worked by Bournemouth based M7 tanks. Here No. 30379 sits in the down bay at Wareham with the 1.03 pm push pull train to Swanage on Friday, 27th July 1962. The Vauxhall Velox car in the yard would be a classic today but was common then. The branch is now connected to the main line again and in the summer of 2018 South Western Railway ran a through train from Salisbury and Weymouth and a shuttle service during the day.

It's 7.35 am on the cold morning of Saturday 18th April as graffiti-adorned Q class 0-6-0 No. 30546 arrives at Wareham with the 7.15 am Swanage to Bournemouth West, which I caught before riding the 'Royal Wessex' to London behind No. 35028 *Clan Line*. I had gone down on the 1.10 am to Salisbury behind No. 35013 *Blue Funnel* and then the 3.17 am to Weymouth via Fordingbridge and Wimborne with BR Standard class four 2-6-0 No. 76018, and finally to Wareham on the 6.35 am from Weymouth with the same engine. 76010 is on the 7.10 am Bournemouth Central to Weymouth though I don't know why it's in the Swanage bay, unless it dropped coaches for a later train onto the branch. Both of the lines via Wimborne would close on 2nd May so my journey on the 3.17 from Salisbury was quite close to the end.

After leaving Wareham on Friday 27th July 1962 (page 143) we caught the 1.27 pm to Upwey behind No. 76069 and spent some time taking photos on the climb out of Weymouth. It was a cloudy and cool day and this shot of rebuilt West Country class pacific No. 34001 *Exeter* on the late running 4 pm Weymouth Quay to Waterloo 'Channel Islands Express' was about the best of a poor bunch of shots. Notice the beautiful old lamp and signs by the crossing. We spent that night camped by the line at Templecombe ready for a summer Saturday on the Somerset and Dorset.

Moving now to the line from Basingstoke to Exeter this shot is taken at Andover Junction on Thursday, 23rd April 1964. It shows rebuilt West Country class pacific No. 34004 *Yeovil* arriving on the 10.54 am semi fast service from Waterloo to Salisbury. On the right is the platform for trains to Andover Town and Romsey which line was known as 'The Sprat and Winkle'. It closed to passengers on 7th September 1964. Note the old hand cart apparently condemned but still in use. 34004 lasted to the end of steam on 9th July 1967.

This was the view seen on alighting from the down 'Atlantic Coast Express' at Salisbury on Saturday, 18th April 1964. The engine is rebuilt Merchant Navy class pacific No. 35016 *Elders Fyffes* and driver Cox of Salisbury shed had just brought the 12 coach train down from Waterloo in 81 minutes for the 83.7 miles which included a speed restriction for track work at Hurstbourne and a signal check at Tunnel Junction; a very fine run. The engine is in superb condition and a tribute to the cleaning staff at Nine Elms in this last year of the ACE. I had caught the train after arriving at Waterloo at 10.50 am on the up 'Royal Wessex'. (see page 144).

Yeovil Junction, 124 miles from Waterloo, is the location for this shot taken on Saturday, 27th June 1964. The train is the 10.35 am Waterloo to Padstow and Bude which was booked first stop Salisbury in 90 minutes then fast to Axminster. Passengers for Padstow wouldn't arrive until 5 pm. The train is hauled by rebuilt West Country class pacific No. 34036 *Westward Ho* and is comprised entirely of Bulleid stock. On the right is a good friend with whom I spent the day. He knew a thing or two about Bulleid's pacifics as his job was to identify and solve problems with them by travelling with the crews. Note the gas lamps on the platform. The tea rooms on the up platform made the best cuppa on the Southern, a tradition which continues to this day.

Very little is now left of Seaton Junction station, seen here on the beautiful morning of Wednesday, 25th July 1962. BR Standard class three 2-6-2 tank No. 82010 is shunting wagons on the up fast line. 82010 had arrived at 8.03 am from Seaton double headed with M7 class 0-4-4 tank No. 30125. We had travelled on this train from Colyford having camped overnight in a field near the line. After photographing more trains we caught the 10.17 am to Exeter Central which was the 8.10 am stopping service from Salisbury. It was hauled by No. 34059 *Sir Archibald Sinclair*, now preserved on the Bluebell Railway.

Soon after we had arrived at Exeter Central, Ivatt class two 2-6-2 tank No. 41304 coupled onto the back of our train to remove some coaches, though the rest of the train would continue at 11.27 am to Ilfracombe Light Pacific in original condition. Then with a crescendo of noise a heavy freight stormed up the hill from Exeter St Davids with Maunsell N class Mogul No. 31820 as train engine piloted by Z class 0-8-0 tank No. 30950. The eight engines of this class were introduced in 1929, designed by Richard Maunsell specifically for heavy yard shunting. By 1960 the entire class had been transferred to Exmouth Junction for banking and pilot work on the 1-in-37 gradient. They were all withdrawn at the end of 1962 when the Western Region took over the lines west of Salisbury and replaced them with Pannier tanks.

Exeter Central a week earlier, on Thursday 19th July 1962, sees the last of the Bulleid light pacifics No 34110 *66 Squadron*, still in original condition, climbing the 1-in-37 into the station. The train is the four coach rear part of the 2.30 pm to Waterloo which had started from Torrington at 12.13 pm. The signalman is about to give the 2-1 train out of section signal to St David's. I had arrived behind No. 35014 *Nederland Line* on the down 'Atlantic Coast Express' and would return to London on the 4.30 pm train behind No. 35001 *Channel Packet*.

Ilfracombe, 226½ miles from Waterloo, and at 3.55 pm, the end of our journey from Waterloo on the 'Atlantic Coast Express' on Monday, 23rd July 1962. As far as Exeter Central our locomotive had been No. 35014 *Nederland Line* which was in fine form giving us a time of 76 minutes 2 seconds for the 83.7 miles to Salisbury. We then had No. 34076 *41 Squadron* from Exeter Central to Ilfracombe. Here the engine was turned on the turntable out of sight beyond the little shed on the left of the picture before taking us back to Yeoford on the 4.50 pm train.

One of our little group's objectives with our Southern Rail rover in July 1962 was to see the Beattie Well tanks working at Wadebridge. To that end on Monday 23rd July having travelled down to Ilfracombe on the 'Atlantic Coast Express' we made our way to Halwill Junction where we camped on the roadside. The next day we caught the 7.15 am to Wadebridge where on our arrival and to our great delight we found 30586 and 30587 both working. 0298 class 2-4-0 WT No. 30586 was built in June 1874 by Beyer Peacock Ltd, withdrawn in December 1962 and scrapped in March 1964. 30587 and the other engine, 30585, not seen that day, are both preserved.

I am finishing this book with three shots from one of my most enjoyable days on the lineside at one of my most frequented and favourite places: Pirbright on the South Western main line thirty miles from Waterloo near the summit of the climb out of London. The date is Sunday 2nd September 1962 and my brothers and I stayed there all day from about 9.30 am until 7 pm. This first photo shows LN class 4-6-0 No. 30861 *Lord Anson* on the SCTS special which has left Waterloo at 9 am destined for Salisbury, the Devon branches and Exeter. This tour was run to commemorate the impending end of this and many other classes of classic Southern steam engines.

The special returned behind N15 class 4-6-0 No. 30770 *Sir Prianius* at about 7.15 pm in the dusk. 30770 was built by the North British Locomotive Company in 1925 and withdrawn two months after this photo was taken. The train had passed milepost 31 at 64 mph and was now running downhill. It had been a perfect day as aside from the usual diet of Bulleid pacifics and Standard class fives a Schools class 4-4-0 had also put in an appearance. No 30925 *Cheltenham* was turned out for the 8.30 am from Plymouth which was due at Waterloo at 3.07 pm after running nonstop up from Salisbury. This train would normally be a Bulleid pacific and I have often wondered if the substitution was contrived in order that all three of the remaining classes of classic main line engines could be seen on the same day before their demise at the year end.

Soon before No. 30770 passed on the SCTS special I got this photo of the up 'Bournemouth Belle'. Rebuilt Merchant Navy pacific No. 35029 *Ellerman Lines* is going well on its 500 ton train with safety valves just feathering; the last of the sun providing glint down the side of the train. This is one of my favourite steam photos and an appropriate way to finish.

Acknowledgements

With thanks to my brothers, especially Bryan (Wedgie) who came with me on many of the long cycle rides and who helped with the lineside vigils. Also to the two Randall brothers, John and Bob, who were with me on some of the rail rovers and who planned and organised our camping stops and kept me going when I flagged. It should be clear from the text where I was accompanied and where I went alone. Finally thanks to my wife for putting up with me spending so many hours on my PC in my study scanning my old negatives, and putting this book together.

Bibliography

British Railway Steam Locomotives 1948-1968 by Hugh Longworth. Ian Allan Publishing.
British Railways Steam Locomotive Allocations by Hugh Longworth. Ian Allan Publishing
The Book of the Merchant Navy Pacifics by Richard Derry. Irwell Press Limited

The Book of the West Country and Battle of Britain Pacifics by Richard Derry. Irwell Press Limited
Steam Locomotives of Great Britain. Locomotion Books
ABC of British Railway Locomotives-Southern Region-summer 1960 edition. Ian Allan Ltd